# THE CLANS AND
# TARTANS OF
# SCOTLAND

R. R. McIAN

INTRODUCTION BY
# ALASTAIR CAMPBELL OF AIRDS, YR.

UNICORN PURSUIVANT

BRACKEN BOOKS
LONDON

PUBLISHED BY BRACKEN BOOKS
AN IMPRINT OF BESTSELLER PUBLICATIONS LTD
PRINCESS HOUSE
50 EASTCASTLE STREET
LONDON W1N 7AP
ENGLAND

*THE CLANS AND TARTANS OF SCOTLAND*
IS A SELECTION OF PLATES FROM
*THE CLANS OF THE SCOTTISH HIGHLANDS*
BY R. R. McIAN
ACKERMANN AND CO.
LONDON
1845

POSTER ART SERIES

*THE CLANS AND TARTANS OF SCOTLAND*
IS A VOLUME IN THE BRACKEN POSTER ART
SERIES. UP TO TEN PLATES MAY BE
REPRODUCED IN ANY ONE PROJECT OR
PUBLICATION, WITHOUT SPECIAL PERMISSION
AND FREE OF CHARGE. WHEREVER POSSIBLE THE
AUTHOR, TITLE AND PUBLISHER SHOULD BE ACKNOWLEDGED
IN A CREDIT NOTE. FOR PERMISSION TO MAKE MORE EXTENSIVE USE
OF THE PLATES IN THIS BOOK APPLICATION
MUST BE MADE TO THE PUBLISHER.

ISBN 1 85170 223 7

PRINTED IN ITALY

# INTRODUCTION

As a nation, we Scots have been quite remarkably successful in projecting an outward image of ourselves around the world. Golf and Scotch whisky have penetrated the furthest corners of the earth; tartan is recurrently top of the fashion parade from Paris to Tokyo. More people wear the kilt today than ever before in history; the martial sound of the Highland pipes is heard across the continents and pipe bands belong to such unexpected military units as the United States Military Academy, West Point, and the Brazilian Marine Corps.

If this export of these essentially Scottish symbols has been successful, there is also much reason to believe that it has in many cases been too successful and we have gone over the top. Take the haggis, for instance, which started life as the desperate attempt of a starving crofter to wring the last scrap of nourishment from a slaughtered beast. Today, at gatherings of Scots all over the world, it is treated with almost religious reverence. It is piped ceremoniously into the room, addressed in the words of our national poet ('Fair fa' your honest sonzie face / Great chieftain o' the Puddin'-race . . .') before being stabbed ceremoniously with a silver mounted dirk, doused in expensive whisky and consumed with (almost) universal relish.

Of all the symbols of Scotland, Highland dress and tartan are among the most powerfully dramatic and romantic. It has been claimed that 'a man in a kilt is a man and a half' and there really is something about the wearing of the kilt that confers extra stature on its owner. It is absolutely no coincidence that the kilted 51st Highland Division was rated by the Germans as the most formidable of all the formations they came across during the First World War. Certainly the British government had no doubts on the matter when, after the defeat of Bonnie Prince Charlie, they banned the use of Highland dress and the tartan, which they clearly saw as an incitement to further subversion. Repeated offenders were sent to the colonies. The form of Highland dress has always owed much to the army and it was the Highland regiments which kept the kilt and the tartan alive until at last, in 1782, their use was once more permitted.

Nowadays, the kilt is seen as the national dress of Scotland. In fact, it started life as no such thing, being entirely confined to the Highlands. The Lowlanders, who have always made up the majority of Scots, regarded what they considered a barbarous form of apparel with loathing and contempt and conferred the opprobrious term of 'redshanks' on the Highlanders, who were, they reckoned, what we would now term 'blue' with cold. But today anyone with the smallest claim to Scots ancestry (and not a few without) proudly wears the kilt; even Lowland chiefs and their followers vie with their Highland counterparts in a way which their forebears would have found incomprehensible and appalling.

The kilt itself in its original form was a very basic garment which required neither the trouble of tailoring nor the frequent replacement which a pair of breeches needed. Two widths of tartan cloth were sewn together to produce the required depth, forming a piece of material some 5 ft wide by 6 yds and more in length. This was known variously as the *Breacan*, the *Feileadh Bhreacain* and the *Feileadh Mor* – the big kilt, usually referred to in English as the belted plaid.

To put it on, its owner put his leather belt on the ground and then placed the material lengthways over it. This he then methodically pleated over the belt until he had gathered along its length all but a couple of feet at either end of the material. Lying down on the belt, he would then fold these ends across his middle before buckling the belt and standing up. The result would not be totally unlike today's kilt; it would hang to just above the knee with pleats at the back and with the front double apron of the kilt relatively flat. Behind him, however, would be all the surplus material from above his belt. He would first put on his waistcoat and jacket and then would gather up all this surplus, tucking it under the skirts of his jacket and his belt and fastening it on his left shoulder, sometimes with an ornamental brooch. The result, properly assembled on a fine figure of a man, could look nothing short of dramatic; on a small dumpy figure it could look a total mess.

But the belted plaid had many advantages in the Highland climate and terrain. It allowed freedom of movement, it was warm, the upper half could provide a voluminous cloak against the weather, it dried out quickly and with much less discomfort than trousers and if required it could, by the mere undoing of the belt, provide very adequate overnight blanketing. When complete freedom of action was required in battle it was easily discarded, and one famous Highland clan battle, that between the Frasers and the MacDonalds and Camerons in 1544, is known as *Blar-na-Leine*, which can be translated as 'Field of the Shirts'.

It appears that the garment was originally largely that of the people; clan chiefs and lesser leaders wore a *Leine Croich* or saffron shirt, in fact a knee-length garment of leather, linen or canvas, heavily pleated and quilted, which provided a surprisingly good defence and which was much more mobile (and less expensive) than contemporary plate armour. This form of dress is to be seen on West Highland tombstones right up to the early seventeenth century, worn with a high conical helmet and the great two-handed claymore.

As it happens, pre-nineteenth century portraits of the chiefs and lairds painted in tartan are remarkably few; in general, apart from those wearing kilted military uniforms, they preferred to have their pictures painted in ordinary dress of the time.

The *Feileadh Beg*, or little kilt, is what we wear today. In essence it consists of the lower part of the old belted plaid with the pleats sewn in at the back and neatly tailored, the ends of the kilt's two aprons being drawn across the front of the body and secured by buckle and strap or by two heavy kilt safety-pins. This form of dress may have existed earlier, but there is no sign of it before 1725. It is a severe shock to many people to find that its originator may well have been an Englishman, one Rawlinson, who was employed as the manager of an iron smelting works in Lochaber who adapted it to allow more freedom of movement for his workers. Be that as it may, it is this form of garment which is now firmly taken as being the kilt.

Myth and misconception also surround the tartan. It is not exclusively Scottish in origin and it can, like bagpipes, be found from the earliest times in many countries around the world. But the use of multi-coloured cloth can be found right back in the earliest days of our Celtic forefathers, when the number of colours was rigorously laid down according to the wearer's rank. There is no doubt that the use of tartan is of very long standing among the Gaels but there is every reason to believe that its general use as a means of identification is of relatively modern origin and cannot go back much beyond the year 1800, if at all.

This is also an area of controversy, but apart from one or two recorded attempts the evidence is overwhelming that before this date, no general clan significance was ascribed to tartan. The widely quoted claim that there were district tartans rests on the report by Martin Martin published in 1703 that it was possible to tell a man's place of origin by the pattern of his plaid. This could well be true in that certain weavers would no doubt make something of a trademark of a tartan that was particularly popular in their locality.

But the evidence for the much later arrival of clan tartan as such is overwhelming and I know of no serious historian who now upholds the romantic claim for an earlier origin. Tartan, anyway, is a hopeless form of identification at any distance, particularly the complicated early patterns; identification was largely due to the wearing of the various clan plant-badges of which, it will be noticed, McIan makes a considerable feature, or by an easily visible token in the bonnet such as the famous Jacobite white cockade. The modern, armorially correct fashion for a clansman of wearing his chief's crest within a buckle and strap displaying the motto as a silver cap-badge can hardly have been general practice as it would have been well beyond the sporrans of most.

Today, tartans abound and it is an unfortunate indeed who will not be told by the tartan shop that he or she indeed can buy 'their' tartan. The ascribing of a vast plethora of names to membership of various clans has long been an industry in itself – luckily there is insufficient space here to enter into that particular subject! But the convention has now been adopted that it is the chief of the clan – assuming that there is one – who lays down who belongs to his clan and what is its tartan.

This transformation of the attitude towards the Highlander in the mind of the rest of the nation from the fear and disgust engendered by the Jacobite rebellions (few people would believe that there were more Scots in arms against Prince Charlie than for him, but such is the case) to admiration and respect is nothing short of remarkable. The bravery of the Highland regiments of the latter part of the eighteenth century must give them the right to claim a large part of the credit, but the early years of the nineteenth century saw the arrival of an extraordinary veneration and romanticizing of the Highlander.

An early influence in this was the tremendous literary impact made by one James Macpherson, who produced a translation of what were claimed to be the heroic poems of Ossian which supposedly dated back to around the third century; in fact Macpherson could never produce the complete Gaelic original and it seems clear that he himself was the author, basing his work, however, on genuine fragments collected from around the Highlands. The scale of this impact may be judged by the fact that Napoleon Bonaparte, no less, carried an edition of Macpherson's works, translated into Italian, across the battlefields of Europe as his favourite bedtime reading and that the name of one of the heroines in these poems, Malvina, was given to a group of islands in the South Atlantic which we know better as the Falklands.

Probably the most potent factor of all in the transformation of the Highlander was the massive output of romantic bestsellers by Sir Walter Scott. Royalty put its seal on the process with the visit to Edinburgh in 1822 by King George IV, the first by a British monarch for close on two centuries. This evoked what can only be described as a theatrical fantasy ably orchestrated by Sir Walter and by Colonel, later General, David Stewart of Garth. Pomp and ceremony were everywhere; 'ancient traditions' were newly invented for the occasion, the traces of which we still see proliferated on every hand today. The whole place was awash with kilted warriors. Even the grotesque figure of Sir William Curtis, Lord Mayor of London, was to be seen swathed in tartan from head to foot in loyal emulation of the monarch. The king's portrait was painted by Sir David Wilkie; he was clad in the garb of Old Gaul with, his detractors claim, the addition of pink tights under his kilt to preserve his modesty and the warmth of his knees. Even if this is mere calumny, it is certainly not beyond a king whose reply to the health drunk in his honour at the most elaborate of official dinners was, with great solemnity, to propose the toast of 'All the chieftains and all the clans of Scotland may God bless the Land of Cakes!'

But the tartan craze was well and truly established and it continued – and indeed continues – to grow. The next arrivals as forces on the scene were the mysterious Sobieski Stuart brothers, who claimed to be the grandsons of Bonnie Prince Charlie. They put on a magnificent charade which took in a number of eminent people; they also were talented artists and produced among other work a book entitled *Vestiarum Scotticum*, supposedly based on an ancient manuscript in their family's possession which, like the original of James Macpherson's verses, could never actually be produced for inspection. The list of what were claimed to be old clan tartans which it contains, although entirely bogus, nevertheless has been taken as the official pattern of many of today's clan setts. The trouble was that the brothers were undoubtedly gifted and some of their work was genuine, although most of it was entirely a product of their fertile imagination. Even McIan was far from free from their influence.

Of course, the most eminent enthusiast of things Highland was Queen Victoria herself, her taste at the time being summed up in that splendid word 'Balmorality'. The Queen displayed enormous pride in her Stewart ancestry, ignoring the fact that if that family had triumphed a hundred years before, her own would have remained in undistinguished obscurity. Her reign saw the final transformation of what their detractors could claim to be a race of savages, however noble, into figures of glamour and romance. The process can perhaps be summed up by the comparison between the silver encrusted and often cairngorm ornamented ceremonial dirk with its knife and fork in the sheath so frequently illustrated here, and the much older and plainer example on display at Inveraray Castle. Any doubt as to the stark purpose of the latter is dispelled by the Gaelic inscription on its worn blade which, being translated, reads 'Give me blood for I am thirsty . . .'.

McIan comes right into the middle of this process and it says much for the quality of his work that it has remained popular for as long as it has. Born in 1803, Robert Ronald McIan started life as an actor, first of all in the West Country, but then in London where he joined the troupe of his friend, the actor William Macready. He produced *The Clans of the Scottish Highlands* in 1845 in conjunction with his great friend James Logan, who wrote the text. The plates reproduced here come from that work. Logan is another colourful figure, his excitable temperament being due, he claimed, to having been struck on the head by a flying hammer into whose path he had walked at a Highland games. His instability led to his being sacked as secretary of that prestigious pressure group, the Highland Society of London, with whom he remained on sufficiently good terms, however, for the Highland Society to underwrite the original publication of the book.

So well were his efforts received, that McIan himself left the stage to devote his life to painting. He and Logan collaborated again in a later work, entitled *The Highlanders at Home or Gaelic Gatherings*. It is sad that his early death in 1856 has prevented us seeing more of his work, which has, however, been preserved in a remarkable fashion.

Being on the stage has undoubtedly contributed to the dramatic way in which he has presented many of his figures. Either he or Logan had obviously studied the subject, but he is not above investing some of his figures with a distinctly theatrical air with which, by now, the whole perception of the Highlander was heavily surrounded. There are one or two obvious anomalies, and on occasion he is not above falling into the trap for the unwary illustrator of depicting sporrans and dirks apparently floating in the air without any form of attachment and suspension. His portrayal of tartan is on the whole pretty good although these pictures are not really ideal for that purpose. I suspect that he has found the painting of Highland weapons irresistible; a number of subjects are girt around with swords, dirks and pistols and would have got terribly in the way had their owners worn them as shown. But that again was typical of the element of dressing up so popular in his time.

That element of fantasy is still with us today now that Highland dress is popular as never before. And yet, in spite of all the razzmatazz, all the nonsense talked and the myths repeated as gospel, there is something that is very special indeed about the kilt and the tartan. It is a limp back indeed that does not straighten as the kilt is buckled on and a poor heart that is not lifted just a little at the sight of what are now taken to be the colours of the clan. The kilt has now become beyond any doubt the national dress of Scotland; let us keep it that way and ensure it is not allowed to decline into mere fancy dress.

ALISTAIR CAMPBELL OF AIRDS, THE YOUNGER
UNICORN PURSUIVANT
APRIL 1988

# BUCHANAN.

London. Ackermann & Co. 96, Strand
C.Graf, Lith to Her Majesty

## PLATE 1

*Buchanan*

*McIan may have meant this to be a picture of an earlier period, but the shape of the sporran, the moustaches and haircut and the ornamental* sgian dubh *or black knife thrust in the right stocking are all nineteenth rather than eighteenth century in feeling. The kilt is the modern form, with a very dramatic use of the plaid, secured across the shoulders by the ornamental silver brooch which often boasts a cairngorm in its centre.*

CAMERON.

R.R. McIan, pinxit.

L. Dickinson, Lith.

London. Ackermann & Cᵒ 96, Strand.

## PLATE 2

### *Cameron*

*A fine figure of a mid-eighteenth-century gentleman wearing the great belted plaid which virtually hides the sporran and dirk around his middle. He is further armed with the Highland broadsword and carries a fine fowling-piece. Note the ornamental knot on his scarlet garters, a form of decoration much cultivated in the latter half of the century.*

R.R. Mc Ian, pinxit.

L. Dickinson, Lith.

CAMPBELL OF ARGYLE.

London, Ackermann & Cº 96 Strand

PLATE 3

*Campbell of Argyll*

*The subject is wearing the proper form of trews – a term now applied to any form of tartan trouser. This form is a tight-fitting one-piece garment – exactly like a modern pair of tights. This type of dress was often adopted by the gentry; they would find it better for riding than the kilt, which is decidedly uncomfortable on horseback. The tartan here, alas, is a Sobieski Stuart invention. The brothers persuaded the sixth Duke of Argyll that he should wear it instead of the plain Black Watch or Campbell pattern worn both by his predecessors and successors, which has misled practically every writer on tartan since. Logan says the subject is reading the Good Book; my friends tell me he is checking out the rent book to see whom he can oppress next. I am not too happy about the Inverness flaps to his tunic which are surely a ninteenth-century invention.*

R.R. McIan, pinxit.

W. Kinnebrook, lith.

**CHISHOLM.**

London: Ackermann & Co. 96, Strand.

PLATE 4

*Chisholm*

*This is in fact a contemporary portrait of
The Chisholm – the clan chief – in full court
dress. He wears a cut-down version of the
Feileadh Mor or belted plaid gathered up
and secured by the brooch on his left shoulder;
he is fully armed with sword, dirk and
pistols. In his bonnet, which is an early form
of the Glengarry, note the three eagle's
feathers of a chief and the fern plant-badge
of his clan.*

COLQUHON.

R.R.M<sup>c</sup>Ian, pinxit.

L. Dickinson, Lith.

London. Ackermann & C<sup>o</sup> 96, Strand.

## PLATE 5

### Colquhoun

*Again, here are the trews as worn by gentle-men in the Highlands. Logan says that the model for the jacket comes from a portrait of Prince Charlie. The plaid is secured on the shoulder to leave both arms free. The tartan is not a particularly good representation, but there is a splendid movement about the figure, which is lively in the extreme. I wonder why he has his dirk under his coat instead of outside it?*

FARQUHARSON.

PLATE 6

*Farquharson*

*The model for this picture fought at Culloden at the age of 115, having also fought with Montrose a century earlier! The tartan is one which was not associated with the clan until much later, but he presents a magnificent figure with his Lochaber axe whose hook allowed you to drag a horseman from the saddle before doing him no good at all with the sharp end.*

FERGUSON.

PLATE 7

*Ferguson*

*I think McIan has got a bit confused here; the picture is said to show the* Leine Croich, *the war coat worn by the gentlemen of the clan up to the early seventeenth century which came well below the knee and whose quilted pleats gave good protection against a sword cut. The helmet should be much more conical in shape and the coat stiff and regular; this is in fact an ordinary belted plaid. I suspect the Sobieski Stuarts may be responsible.*

FORBES.

R.R. McIan, pinxit.　　　　　L. Dickinson, lith.

London Ackermann & Cº 96, Strand.

## PLATE 8

### Forbes

*A splendid full Highland court dress of Bonnie Prince Charlie's period. As well as the eagle feathers of the chief, the bonnet displays a sprig of broom, the plant-badge of the Forbes's. The tartan jacket and waist-coat are heavily gold laced and a pistol is stuck in the sword-belt. I am not entirely happy about the use of the plaid brooch at this period and, of course, the clan tartan is of a later date.*

F R A S E R.

## PLATE 9
### *Fraser*

*A distinctly Byronic representation of a Fraser chieftain, shown wearing an early form of the nineteenth-century Glengarry, which is a cut-down version of the old bonnet and is an ornamental rather than a practical head-dress. The sporran is also nineteenth century. McIan has slipped into a common fault here; the dirk is suspended in mid-air – it should be attached to a strap suspended from the waistbelt.*

R.R. Mᶜ Ian, pinxit.                                    W. Posley, Lit.

GORDON.

PLATE 10

*Gordon*

*The kilt is adequate for fishing, provided you don't have to wade up to your waist; in that case it floats around you on the water, which can be embarrassing as well as getting in the way. This is a contemporary picture (i.e. c. 1840). The Gordon tartan shown here is one of several clan tartans which have a military origin: here the basic Black Watch sett with the addition of the yellow facing stripe of the regiment. I bet this chap's wife gave him hell when he got home for spoiling his nice velvet jacket with smelly fish-scales — worth it, though, for two fine salmon!*

# GRAHAM.

London. Ackermann & C<sup>o</sup> 96, Strand.

PLATE 11

## Graham

*This is said to be either a ghillie or a shepherd dressed for the hill; he looks too smart for either of these, I reckon; at least, I think he would have left his fine sporran behind. His dirk is a plain one without the knife and fork, which are often carried on the sheath. Again, McIan has slipped up in leaving it without any means of support; even Homer nods! His hose are cut from cloth on the slant, the old practice; they would not have maintained their shape as well as the later knitted stockings.*

R.R. M<sup>c</sup> Ian, pinxit.

Louis Dickinson Lith.

GRANT.

London. Ackermann & Co. 96, Strand.

Graf. Lith. to Her Majesty.

PLATE 12

*Grant*

*The results of a good day on the hill after black game; this lad carries his employer's gun and the bag, some of it wrapped in his plaid. The blackcock's tail-feathers are much used by military pipers to adorn their Glengarries.*

R.R.M<sup>c</sup> Ian, pinxit

M & N. Hanhart, Imp<sup>t</sup>

GUNN.

London: Published by Ackermann & C<sup>o</sup> 96 Strand

PLATE 13
*Gunn*

*A good representation of the* Feileadh Mor *seen from the rear, with the spare material gathered on the left shoulder where it was usually attached by a bow of ribbon rather than the later plaid brooch of the nineteenth century. The bonnet here is of the eighteenth-century pattern with a red band around it. This was an alternative to the plain blue bonnet or the variety with a diced band, which are now the more usual patterns.*

R.R. Mc Ian, pinxit.

L. Dickinson, Lith.

J. Macalister
Passenger
Canada

MACALISTER.

London. Ackermann & Cº 96. Strand.

PLATE 14

*Macailaster*

*Much has been made of the Highland Clearances – the period during which the lairds encouraged their people, forcibly at times, to seek fresh fortune overseas. In fact many went gladly with assistance from their landlords and the sad fact is that the whole thing was inevitable sooner or later. The Highlands, beautiful as they are, are also cruelly ineffective in supporting more than a limited population at little above subsistence level.*

R. R. McIan, pinxit.

L. Dickinson, Lith.

MAC AULAY.

London, Ackermann & Co. 96, Strand.
Printed by C Graf.

PLATE 15

*Macaulay*

*The kilt – here shown with a separate plaid – is a remarkably good cold-weather garment. The vital middle of the body is covered by several layers of material and bare knees are remarkably impervious to cold. The plaid makes an enveloping cloak whose insulation can actually be improved when it is wet. It is in hot countries that the kilt can be really uncomfortable and there an alternative form of dress is far preferable.*

Mar Chuimhneachan air
Clann Dónuill Ghlinne Comhan
a mhurtadh anns an oidhche
de an Fhaoilteach 1692 a reir
ordugh Righ Villiam III air
am beil cuimhne bheannaichte

R.R.McIan, pinxit.

L. Dickinson, Lith.

MACDONALD OF GLENCO.

London. Ackermann & Co 96, Strand.

PLATE 16

*MacDonald of Glencoe*

*The Massacre of Glencoe is one of the biggest misconceptions of Highland history. It was not an act of clan vengeance by the Campbells on the MacDonalds but a deliberate act of government policy carried out under orders by a red-coated government regiment – the Earl of Argyle's – against a clan whose chief had failed to sign the Oath of Allegiance by the required time. But, as so often, the myth is much less fun than the truth in the popular mind.*

R R Mc Ian, pinxit.

W. Bosley, Lith.

MACDUFF.

London Ackermann & Co 96. Strand.

PLATE 17
*MacDuff*

*This fearsome figure is wearing 'moggans' or footless stockings. In fact, in battle, the Highlander was wont to shed his large belted plaid and fight in his shirt alone, to allow complete freedom of movement. He would tie the ends of his shirt together for the sake of modesty – hence the famous battle between the Frasers and the Camerons and MacDonalds in 1544 known as* Blar-na-Leine *or* 'Field of the Shirts'.

# MAC DUGAL.

London. Ackermann, & C<sup>o</sup> 96, Strand.

C. Graf, Lith. to Her Majesty.

PLATE 18
*MacDugal*

*There is no evidence of the use of the little kilt – the garment in use today – before 1725. The sporran and dirk are authentic mid-eighteenth century but I cannot see how the kilt is being kept up! It is much too early for the strap and buckles of today and there is no sign of the heavy pins which are an alternative. The sword is the proper claymore of an earlier age – a fearsome weapon which, however, left its wielder without a shield.*

MACGREGOR.

PLATE 19

*MacGregor*

*This dramatic figure is said to be swearing vengeance against the Campbells. In fact the MacGregors had made such a literally bloody nuisance of themselves in the West Highlands that the Crown proscribed the whole clan. At one time they all had a price on their heads and were hunted by all and sundry. Their lands taken from them, they wandered the hills under the romantic sounding but ultimately desperate name of 'The Children of the Mist'.*

MAC INNES.

London Ackermann & Co. 96, Strand.

### PLATE 20

*MacInnes*

*An early warrior under pressure: it is to be hoped that his chain-mail tunic gives him more effective protection than his targe or shield. His own weapon is the short spear so often depicted on early West Highland tombstones. One can appreciate how the Highlander received the old opprobious epithet of 'redshank', although we would say they were 'blue' with cold.*

MAC INTOSH.

R. R. Mᶜ Ian, pinxit.

L. Dickinson, Lith.

London. Published by Ackermann & Co, 96, Strand.

## PLATE 21
### MacIntosh

*From the three eagle feathers in his bonnet along with the plant-badge of red whortle-berry, this must be The Mackintosh himself, the chief of the great Clan Chattan confeder-ation of clans that claimed a distant descent from the early Dalriadic kings of Argyll. He is magnificently clad in the court dress of the early eighteenth century. This is an excellent representation of the* Feileadh Mor *or belted plaid.*

R.R. M⁰Ian, pinxit

L. Dickinson, Lith.

## MAC KAY.

London. Ackermann, & Co. 96, Strand.

## PLATE 22
### MacKay

*Sitting in the kilt is an art that requires constant attention; this gentleman passes — just. His shield is the typical eighteenth-century round targe, whose central spike enabled it to be used for offence as well as defence. His brogues or shoes are made from deerskin and the method of lacing them is still to be seen on occasion with certain patterns of shoes worn with Highland dress today.*

R.R. Mc Ian, pinxit.

L Dickinson Lith.

MACKENZIE.

## PLATE 23
### MacKenzie

*This Jacobite supporter (note the white cockade or bunch of ribbons in his bonnet) is in an uncomfortable situation; his pursuers are apparently Highlanders like himself — probably his ancient enemies, the Macleods, who along with most of the Northern Highland clans turned out for King George. A little known fact is that there were actually more Scots in arms against Prince Charlie than for him. The tartan is military in origin and from a later date.*

MACKINNON.

## PLATE 24

*MacKinnon*

*I fear this Victorian gentleman is indulging in a bit of romanticism! His plaid is arranged to resemble the old big kilt and the cuffs of his velvet jacket date from an earlier time, but the sporran and the mutton-chop whiskers are a giveaway! The longbow is still the principal weapon carried by the Queen's bodyguard for Scotland. The Royal Company of Archers and, in expert hands, is not to be underestimated as a weapon of war.*

MACLACHLAN.

London. Ackermann & Co. 96, Strand.

## PLATE 25
### MacLachlan

*I suspect this is one of the more authentic figures for the Jacobite period; certainly the sporran, if worn, would be of this pattern, a simple leather pouch with drawstrings and often a metal cantle, or top. The sett of the tartan is of a later date. Note the waistcoat and brogues, both made out of deerskin with the hair still on it.*

MAC LEAN.

London, Ackermann & Co. 96 Strand.

## PLATE 26

### MacLean

*This is said to be the Hebridean Chieftain Maclean of Coll. As I go to stay with a descendant of his who has bought and magnificently restored his ancestor's castle on this windswept isle, I had better not be too rude about the fact that his forebear has promoted himself to three feathers instead of the two which better befit his status, and restrain myself as to the theatrical nature of his jacket which smacks of a Sobieski Stuart fantasy!*

R.R.McIan, pinxit.

L.Dickinson, Lith.

MAC LENNAN.

London. Ackermann & Co. 96, Strand.

## PLATE 27
### *MacLennan*

*An excellent depiction of the use of the upper part of the belted plaid in bad weather. When nightfall came, the Highlander had merely to undo his belt to become enveloped in his nightwear/bed clothes in an extremely effective fashion. The reconstruction of the kilt the next morning, however, with the need for all that careful folding of the pleats, must have been a considerable bore.*

## MACLEOD

London. Published by Ackermann & Co. 96 Strand

## PLATE 28
*MacLeod*

*The belted plaid well put on a tall figure could look magnificent, as is clearly shown here; on a small dumpy figure one is told it could look a mess. The tartan is of late-eighteenth-century military origin, being the basic government or Black Watch sett with the addition of red and white lines. McIan has been confused by the title of Lord Macleod, who raised the 71st (later 73rd) Highlanders in 1777. He was in fact a Mackenzie, which clan later adopted this pattern.*

# MAC MILLAN.

London Ackermann & Cº 96, Strand.

## PLATE 29
### MacMillan

*One theory which raises instant wrath north of the border is that the little kilt as shown here and worn today was invented by an Englishman, one Rawlinson, who was manager of the iron smelting works in Lochaber in the early eighteenth century. Be that as it may, there is no record of the little kilt as early as Cromwellian times, and the gaudy tartan is, I think I am right in suggesting, yet another confection of the egregious brothers Sobieski Stuart!*

TOUGH AT THE CAT BOT A GLOVE.

MACPHERSON.

PLATE 30
*MacPherson*

*This is a somewhat theatrical figure of the mid-nineteenth century in full Highland dress – which was fully acceptable, incidentally, as court dress. From the inscription on the pistol butts it is Cluny himself, the title by which the chief of the Macphersons is known. The white cockade in his bonnet would have been somewhat tactless at Court even though Queen Victoria took great pride in her Stuart ancestry.*

MAC RAE.

London, Ackermann & Co 96 Strand

PLATE 31
*MacRae*

*A Victorian ghillie or stalker carries the
hind that has just been shot. Many Highland
estates outfitted their people in the kilt
although tweed plus-fours were in general the
most popular garb, as they remain today;
the kilt is not ideal for crawling in. The
tartan has an obvious link with the Mackenzie sett, the MacRaes having long been loyal
followers of that clan, from which they were
known as 'Mackenzie's Shirt of Mail'.*

MENZIES.

London Ackermann & Co.96 Strand

PLATE 32

*Menzies*

*This figure would seem to date from around the early 1800s – any claim to its being earlier does not fit with the shape of the sporran or the subject's whiskers. The bonnet is the old blue Hummle bonnet 'cocked' in the military fashion which, with the addition of ever more feathers, eventually became the military feather bonnet. This one displays the black cockade of a Hanoverian supporter.*

R.R. M<sup>c</sup> Ian, pinxit.

L. Dickinson, Lith.

MUNRO.

London, Ackermann & C.º 96, Strand.

PLATE 33

*Munro*

*A contemporary seated figure of McIan's own period which, although it has no specific features, none the less shows well the formation of the kilt and plaid. The Munros, like other clans in the same position, sometimes wear the government or Black Watch tartan, having been much involved with that unit's early days.*

R.R.M.ᶜIan, pinxit.

L. Dickinson, Lith.

MURRAY.

PLATE 34

*Murray*

*A fine figure of a Jacobite warrior. The wearing of the clan plant-badge in the bonnet together with the cockade of one's political allegiance was obviously much more prevalent in early days than our present fashion of wearing a metal badge of the chief's crest within a buckled strap.*

OGILVIE.

## PLATE 35
### Ogilvie

*McIan hasused a contemporary portrait by Allan Ramsay of the Third Duke of Perth, a Jacobite commander who was mortally wounded at Culloden, which he has dressed up as an Ogilvie; the details of the dress are therefore entirely authentic. The figure shows the trews being worn in conjunction with a plaid thrown around the shoulders. He has, however, added the two pistols in the sword-belt.*

R.R. Mᶜ Ian, pinxit.

W. Kinnebrook, lith.

ROBERTSON.

PLATE 36
*Robertson*

*McIan apparently took this figure from a sketch of a Highland gentleman who resided at the Court of Louis XIV (1643–1715) where he used to appear in the Highland garb to general admiration. There is therefore a slight air of overdressing about the figure, but it does show how the dress of most ages can be effectively combined with the kilt – in this case the full belted plaid.*

ROSS.

## PLATE 37
### Ross

*A distinctly elaborate costume in which to go shooting on the hill. The elaborate hair sporran came in in the 1770s or thereabout and was much more of an ornament than the utilitarian leather pouch it succeeded; this shape is not seen earlier than well into the nineteenth century; it and the sword would get horribly in the way but our hero has at least bagged a brace of ptarmigan, these attractive partridge-like birds usually found above 2000 ft which go white in winter to merge with the snow.*

London, Ackermann & Co. 96, Strand.

R.R. M<sup>c</sup> Ian, pinxit.

W. Bosley, Lith.

SINCLAIR.

London. Ackermann & Co 96, Strand.

## PLATE 38
### *Sinclair*

*A Highland girl clad in an* arisaid *or shawl of tartan; the snood binding her hair, is, says Logan, an indication of unmarried status. The Highland male being more gaudy in his plumage than the female, womens'* arisaids *were often largely undyed white or grey which, it is claimed, is the basis of the modern gaudy dress tartans of today so beloved of professional Highland dancers and tourists alike.*

STEWART.

R.R. McᶜIan. pinxit.                                    J. Dickinson, Lith.

S T E W A R T.

London Ackermann, & Cᵒ 96, Strand.

## PLATE 39

*Stewart*

*Himself, Bonnie Prince Charlie in person, who was much given to wearing the Highland dress, here shown with the ribbon and star of the Garter. For one who obviously had much charisma as a young man, his later life was a sad comedown and gives us the impression that it was indeed fortunate for us that he never gained the throne.*

R R M┄an, pinxit.

L. Dickinson, Lith.

SUTHERLAND.

London. Ackermann & C⁰ 6 Strand.

PLATE 40

*Sutherland*

*This figure is meant for a shepherd searching for his flock. It is contemporary with McIan and has splendid life to it. The Sutherlands are one of the clans which wear the Black Watch or government tartan on occasion, owing to early military connections – it was worn as early as 1756 by the Sutherland Fencibles and later by the famous 93rd, The Sutherland Highlanders, who formed the Thin Red Line at Balaklava.*